I ♥ BEER!

An Odd Squad book about the world of MEN
by Allan Plenderleith

ℛℛ
RAVETTE PUBLISHING

First Published by
Ravette Publishing Limited 2005
Unit 3, Tristar Centre, Star Road, Partridge Green,
West Sussex RH13 8RA

Printed and bound in Malta

ISBN: 1 84161 238 3

The morning after, Jeff's mouth felt like
he'd licked a badger's arse.

Once again, Alf spent the night
"on the piss".

Realising that cleavages always get served
first at the bar, Jeff takes some action.

Arriving home late after a night out with
the lads, Jeff had a feeling Maude was
in a bit of a huff.

Upon reflection, perhaps the best place for a dartboard *wasn't* beside an open window.

Little did Maude know, Jeff's 'buns of steel'
were actually two carefully concealed colanders.

Jeff had picked his nose a bit too deeply that time.

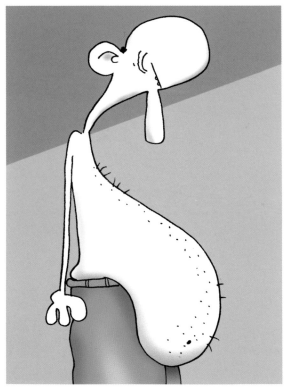

The morning after, Jeff woke up
with a terrible hangover.

After a few drinks, Dug would usually end up
in bed with some fat bird.

Embarrassed by his balding,
Jeff had decided to get hair plugs.

To drag Jeff away from the games console,
Maude dressed up in something irresistible.

Jeff discovers his DIY winter hot tub for
tiny helpless birds is clearly faulty.

Jeff had no need for women - not since he'd developed his very own set of 'beer boobs'.

MENTAL AGILITY

IF YOU MIX ONE PART VODKA WITH 2 PARTS GIN, THREE PARTS WHISKY, A DASH OF LIME AND A CHERRY, WHAT DO YOU GET?

1 x   2 x

3 x

+ 🍋 + 🍒 = ?

ANSWER:
A bloody awful hangover

FOOD

WHICH OF THESE MEALS LOOKS APPEALING TO YOU....?

Fish + Chips

= SOBER-ISH

Vindaloo

= HAD A FEW!

Deep Fried Pizza

= SOZZLED!

Kebab

= MULLERED!

SEX APPEAL TEST
WHICH OF THESE LOVELY LADIES LOOKS SEXY TO YOU?

= SOBER

= TIPSY

= SOZZLED

= COMPLETELY HAMMERED!

At the weekend, Jeff drinks like a fish.

Dug finally figures out a way to get
Debbie to go "down south".

Jeff likes to hang out with his mates
down the pub.

Jeff got the feeling the barman was using
Harry Potter mania to his advantage.

Cool! His master had left him a vegetable curry on the floor - AND it was warm!

eff always made sure he ate the recommended
5 portions of vegetables a day.

That would be the last time Jeff would
utter the words "Keep the noise down -
I'm watching the footie".

Dug's indian takeaway came with a free nan.

Maude was about to say how nice the new jacuzzi was, when she noticed something.

Once again, Jeff had spent the
weekend getting lashed.

How to have the perfect LAD'S NIGHT OUT!

1. PLAY THE CORNY CHAT-UP LINE GAME. THE GUY WHO GETS THE MOST SLAPS WINS!

2. DRINK MORE THAN YOUR BODY WEIGHT IN ALCOHOL!

. FLASH YOUR BUM TO AS MANY PEOPLE AS POSSIBLE!

BOKE!

4. FINISH THE NIGHT BY PUKING UP IN A TAXI!

As the drunken Jeff aims the key for the 2015th time, he slowly begins to weep.

As she climbed the ladder, Jeff got a glimpse of Brenda's huge muff.

As a sexy treat, Jeff asked Maude to
wear her Panty Hose.

Jeff meets his ideal woman - dressed from head to toe in leather!

Being a mechanic began to affect
Jeff's performance in the bedroom.

Sexually frustrated, Jeff had to resort to spanking the monkey.

Dug makes the common mistake of going
for a pee immediately after sex.

It wasn't so much the poo in his slipper that bothered Jeff - more the smirk on the dog's face.

This wasn't quite what Dug had in mind when h
dreamed of rolling grass for a living.

Jeff was so embarrassed when he realised he answered the door with a 'semi' sticking out.

1. Put SPORT before all else!

2. At the slightest hint of a sniffle, take the day off - it's definitely the FLU!

3. Pretend you're listening to a woman, when actually you're gazing at her baps!

4. Rejoice in anything that comes out of your body that's loud and smelly!

Reserve all your love for your one true love - your car!

Wash only when truly necessary!

Unfortunately, in an effort to smell his own fart, Jeff had bent back too far.

Once again, Jeff woke up with a big stiffy.

TOP TIPS FOR A GOLFER!

1. Always wear snazzy mismatched clothes including the all important jumper with diamonds!

2. Make a hole in your pocket for rolling out a spare golf ball onto the green!

Use clever distraction techniques while you "putt" the ball!

Celebrate your glorious victory with quiet dignity!

AN IMPORTANT GUIDE TO BOGIE PICKING!

1. Before going in for the pick, make sure no-one is around to see the shameful act!

Pull bogie out slowly and carefully: beware of attached nose hairs!

3. Wipe bogie discretely under the arm of the sofa - just beware of 'bogie build-up'!

Alternatively, perform the classic
'Roll and Flick' manoeuvre (just be careful!).

HOW TO PREPARE FOR A STINKING HANGOVER!

1. Make sure the toilet is clearly sign-posted to avoid accidents!

2. Install handle bars to the floor for something to hold onto when the room starts spinning!

3. Keep pets hidden to avoid any drunken romantic errors!

4. Place buckets around the house to collect projectile vomit!

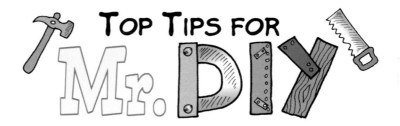

TOP TIPS FOR Mr. DIY

1. Make sure you have all essentials for the job!

Hammer, chisel, twelve cans of lager .... check!

2. Keep the family amused by hurting yourself and swearing loudly!

P*****@*!!!

Mum, what's a "CLUCKING BELL"?

Er, nothing

Appear extra butch by covering your face in grease, making manly grunts and blowing off loudly!

. Cover any dodgy bits of DIY with a selection of household items!

The Odd Squad Guide to GETTING BLADDERED!

1. Don't eat too much before going out - it just takes up valuable space!

2. If the room starts spinning, just spin in the opposite direction!

3. If you don't want to be arrested, try keeping your willy in your trousers!

. If you're going to be sick, DO NOT put your hand over your mouth!

Other ODD SQUAD books available ...

		ISBN	Price
The Odd Squad's Big Poo Handbook	(hardcover)	1 84161 168 9	£7.99
The Odd Squad's Sexy Sex Manual	(hardcover)	1 84161 220 0	£7.99
The Odd Squad Butt Naked		1 84161 190 5	£3.99
The Odd Squad Gross Out!		1 84161 219 7	£3.99
The Odd Squad's Saggy Bits		1 84161 218 9	£3.99
The REAL Kama Sutra		1 84161 103 4	£3.99
The Odd Squad Volume One		1 85304 936 0	£3.99
I Love Poo!	(hardcover)	1 84161 240 5	£4.99
I Love Sex!	(hardcover)	1 84161 241 3	£4.99
I Love Wine!	(hardcover)	1 84161 239 1	£4.99
The Odd Squad's Little Book of Booze		1 84161 138 7	£2.50
The Odd Squad's Little Book of Men		1 84161 093 3	£2.50
The Odd Squad's Little Book of Oldies		1 84161 139 5	£2.50
The Odd Squad's Little Book of Poo		1 84161 096 8	£2.50
The Odd Squad's Little Book of Pumping		1 84161 140 9	£2.50
The Odd Squad's Little Book of Sex		1 84161 095 X	£2.50
The Odd Squad's Little Book of Women		1 84161 094 1	£2.50
The Odd Squad's Little Book of X-Rated Cartoons		1 84161 141 7	£2.50

HOW TO ORDER: Please send a cheque/postal order in £ sterling, made payable to 'Ravette Publishing' for the cover price of the books and allow the following for post & packing ...

UK & BFPO	60p for the first book & 30p per book thereafter
Europe & Eire	£1.00 for the first book & 50p per book thereafter
Rest of the world	£1.80 for the first book & 80p per book thereafter

RAVETTE PUBLISHING
Unit 3, Tristar Centre, Star Road, Partridge Green, West Sussex RH13 8RA

Prices and availability are subject to change without prior notice.